# UNITED STATES OF AMERICA

## WORLD ADVENTURES

BY STEFFI CAVELL-CLARKE

BookLife

©2017
Book Life
King's Lynn
Norfolk PE30 4LS

**ISBN:** 978-1-78637-124-9

Written by:
Steffi Cavell-Clarke

Edited by:
Grace Jones

Designed by:
Natalie Carr

A catalogue record for this book
is available from the British Library.

All rights reserved
Printed in Malaysia

# UNITED STATES OF AMERICA

## WORLD ADVENTURES

### CONTENTS

Words in **red** can be found in the glossary on page 24.

# WHERE ARE THE UNITED STATES OF AMERICA?

The United States of America is a country found in North America. It is made up of 50 areas called states.

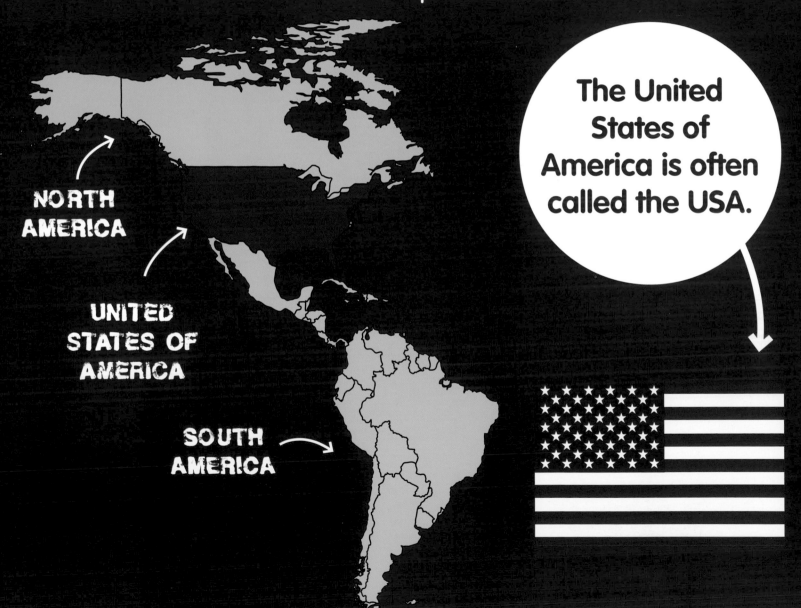

NORTH AMERICA

UNITED STATES OF AMERICA

SOUTH AMERICA

The United States of America is often called the USA.

The **population** of the USA is over 318 million. Many people in the USA live in large cities, such as New York City and Los Angeles.

WASHINGTON, D.C., USA

The capital city of the USA

# WEATHER AND LANDSCAPE

The weather in the USA changes across the country. Some parts of the USA have extreme weather, such as tornadoes.

TORNADO

There are many different types of landscape in the USA. There are mountains, forests and rivers.

The Missouri River is the longest river in the USA.

MISSOURI RIVER, USA

# CLOTHING

In the USA, trainers are called sneakers.

Many people living in the USA dress in cool and comfortable clothing, such as jeans and t-shirts.

Blue jeans are very popular in the USA. They are made from a **material** called denim.

JEANS

# RELIGION

The **religion** with the most followers in the USA is Christianity. Christians celebrate special events throughout the year, such as Christmas.

There are also people in the USA who follow other religions, such as Judaism, Islam and Hinduism.

# FOOD

PASTRY

Apple pie is a popular dish in the USA. It is made from baked apples and pastry.

Hot dogs are also very popular in the USA. A hot dog is a cooked sausage in a sliced bun.

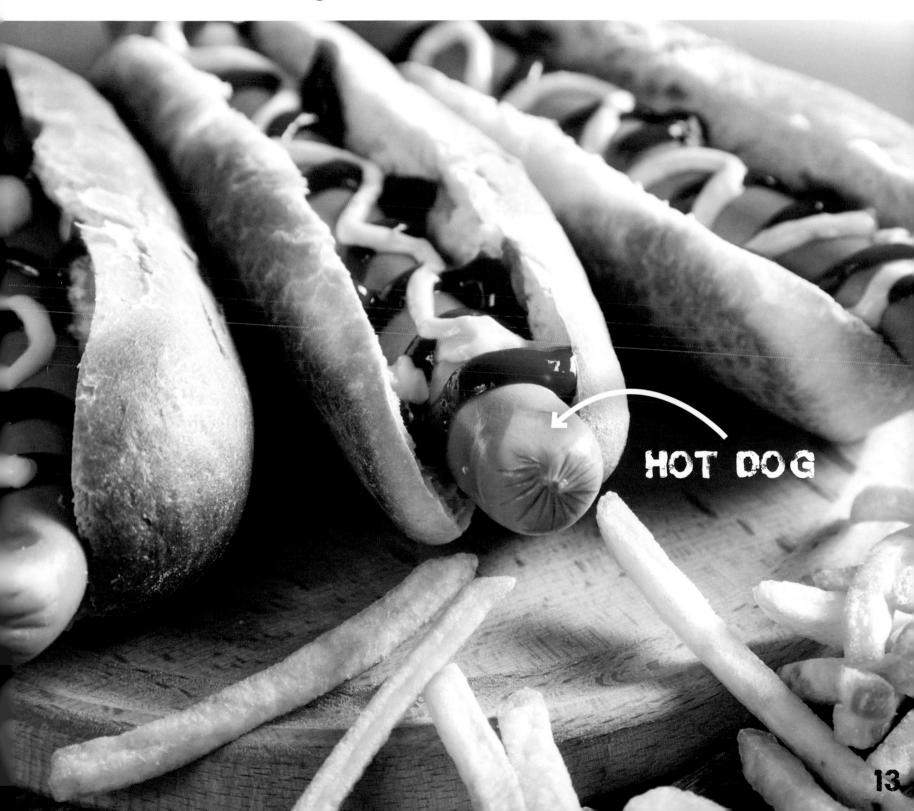

HOT DOG

# AT SCHOOL

Many children in the USA go to **kindergarten** before they start school. In kindergarten, children often learn how to draw, read and write.

After kindergarten, children go to school. They learn subjects such as maths, science, history, geography and English.

# AT HOME

Apartments in New York City, USA.

Many people in the USA live in large cities. In most cities, there are people who live in apartments in tall tower blocks.

In towns and villages, many people live in houses. Many houses built in the USA have porch areas. People often use these to sit on.

PORCH

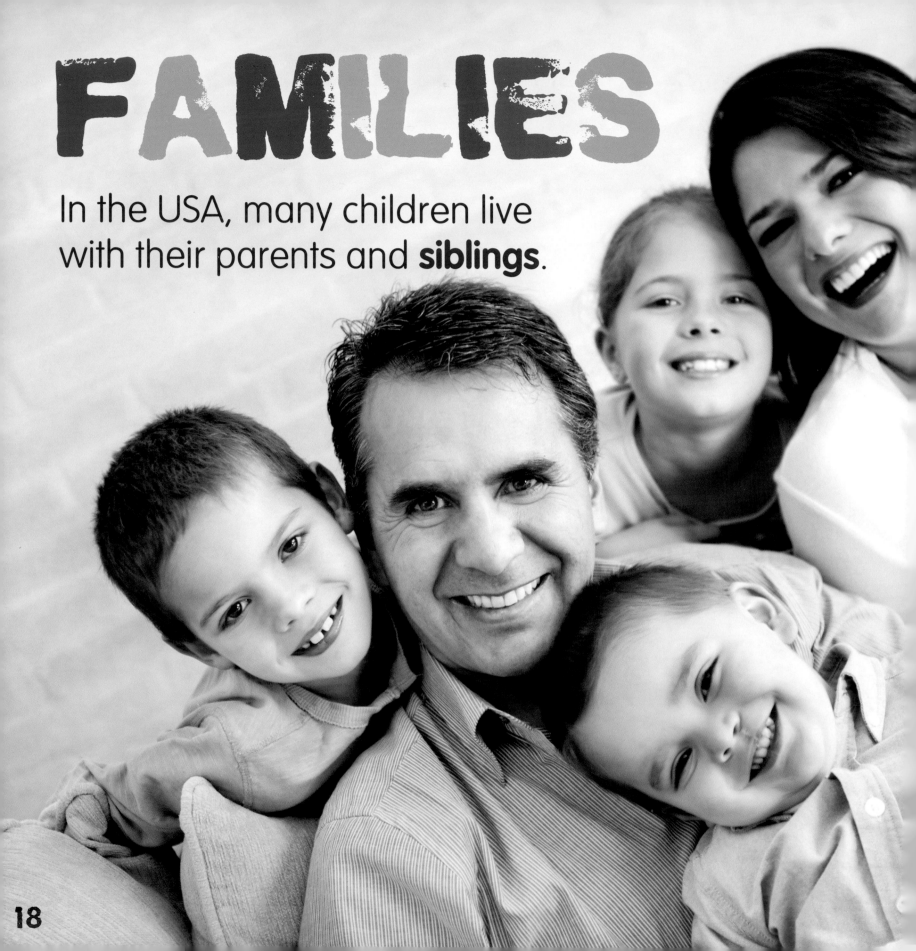

# FAMILIES

In the USA, many children live with their parents and **siblings**.

18

Many families in the USA like to get to together to celebrate special occasions, such as **Thanksgiving**.

SPORT

AMERICAN
FOOTBALL

People in the USA are known for enjoying many
different types of sport. One of the most popular
sports is American football.

Every year a huge American football game, called the Super Bowl, takes place. Thousands of people go to watch.

THE SUPER BOWL

# FUN FACTS

Neil Armstrong was an astronaut from the USA. He was the first person to walk on the moon.

He said "That's one small step for man, one giant leap for mankind".

NEIL ARMSTRONG

There are many cowboys and cowgirls living and working in the USA. They wear special boots and hats and often spend their day riding horses and looking after cows.

# GLOSSARY

**astronaut** someone who is trained to go up into space

**extreme** dangerous and serious

**kindergarten** pre-school

**material** fabric or cloth

**population** number of people living in a place

**religion** the belief in and worship of a god or gods

**siblings** brothers and sisters

**Thanksgiving** a national holiday in the United States of America

**tornadoes** fast-moving, strong winds that form into funnel shapes

# INDEX

**Photocredits: Abbreviations: l-left, r-right, b-bottom, t-top, c-centre, m-middle.**

Front Cover – Samuel Borges Photography. 2 – Sean Pavone. 5 – Orhan Cam. 6 – Minerva Studio. 7 – kavram. 8 – Oleg Mikhaylov. 9 – Lana K. 10 – Pressmaster. 11 – ChameleonsEye. 12 – Africa Studio. 13 – Ruslan Mitin. 14 – Poznyakov. 15 – Pressmaster. 16 – littleny. 17 – Chasecom Media. 18 – Andresr. 19 – Monkey Business Images. 20 – Aspen Photo. 21 – Anthony Correia. 22 background – HelenField. 22 – NASA via Wikimedia 23 – Sorin Colac.